FRUIT AND VEGETABLE SALAD RECIPES

1

INTRODUCTION

THIS BOOK CONTAINS A VARIETY OF RECIPES FOR SALADS REPRESENTING NATIONAL CUISINE OF VARIOUS COUNTRIES. SOME OF THEM ARE EASY TO MAKE AND SOME ARE NOT, BUT IT IS ALWAYS NICE TO COOK SOMETHING NEW, ISN'T IT?

THANKS TO THIS BOOK YOU WILL BE ABLE TO COOK YOUR OWN "HOME-STYLE" AND SURPRISINGLY DELICIOUS SALADS. RECIPES IN THIS BOOK ARE EXCELLENT FOR FESTIVE PARTIES AND FOR TYPICAL HOME LUNCHES AND DINNERS.

I HOPE THESE RECIPES WILL HELP YOU DIVERSIFY YOUR "COOKING" LIFE STARTING FROM TODAY! TREAT YOURSELF, YOUR FRIENDS AND BELOVED ONES!

Fruit Salad ABC

STRAWBERRY
100G

BLUEBERRY
100G

KIWI 2

DRIED DATES
12

CUCUMBER
200G

PAPAYA 100G

CASHEW
NUTS 50G

CHERRY
TOMATO 100G

OLIVE OIL
100 ML

Fruit Salad with Yogurt & Nuts

BANANA 1

KIWI 1

ORANGE 1

APPLE 1

PEAR 1

PLUM 1

RAISINS 50G

DRIED APRICOTS 2

WALNUT 50G

YOGURT 200G

Fruit Salad with Cottage Cheese

BANANA 1

KIWI 1

ORANGE 1

APPLE 1

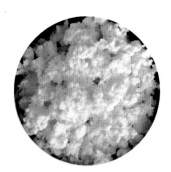

FAT-FREE
COTTAGE CHEESE
150G

YOGURT 150G

Fruit Salad with Kiwi

KIWI 3

TANGERINE 1

HONEY 30G

LEMON JUICE 2 TSP.

PINE NUTS TO TASTE

MINT TO TASTE

Summer Fruit Salad with Yogurt

APPLE 1

PEAR 1

BANANA 2

PEACH 1

GOOSEBERRY
TO TASTE

YOGURT 150G

Fruit Fantasy Salad

MITSUNA
100G

CHARD 100G

OLIVE OIL
50G

ORANGE 1

CANNED
PEACHES
200G

MINT 20G

APPLE 1

STRAWBERRY
100G

PHYSALIS 5

Fruit Salad with Yogurt

BANANA 1

APPLE 1

PEAR 1

STRAWBERRY 100G

YOGURT 150G

Fruit Salad with Mayonnaise

APPLE 3

PEAR 1

ORANGE 1

TANGERINE 1

LEMON 1/4

MAYONNAISE 45G

POWDERED SUGAR 1/2 TSP.

Fruit Salad with Grapes

PEAR 1

APPLE 100G

SUGAR 5G

GRAPES 80G

TANGERINE 1

CANNED PEACHES 100 G

MINT 5G

STRAWBERRY 100G

STRAWBERR Y SYRUP 50ML

YOGURT 150G

Fruit Salad with Red Apples

RED APPLE 2   PEAR 2   ALMOND 45G   BANANA 2

SUGAR 60G   RAISINS 50G   ORANGE 2   BRANDY 45ML

Fruit Chicken Salad with Pineapple

MAYONNAISE 200G

LIME JUICE 2 TSP.

CANNED PINEAPPLE 200G

ORANGE 1

ROASTED PEANUTS 85G

LETTUCE LEAVES TO TASTE

BOILED CHICKEN BREAST FILLET 2

SALT TO TASTE

GROUND BLACK PEPPER TO TASTE

Fruit Salad with Berries & Mint

**STRAWBERRY
200G**

**PINEAPPLE
150G**

**GREEN
APPLE 200G**

**BLACKBERRY
150G**

MINT 15G

Fruit Salad with Chocolate Chips

GRAPES 150G

BANANA 1

KIWI 2

YOGURT 150G

CANNED
PINEAPPLE
100G

CHOCOLATE
CHIPS TO
TASTE

Fruit Salad "Morning"

APPLE 1

BANANA 1

TANGERINE 1

SOUR CREAM 150G

CHOCOLATE CHIPS TO TASTE

COCOA POWDER 1 TSP.

Fruit Salad with *Red Grapes*

RED
GRAPES 150G

WHITE
GRAPES 150G

PLUM 3

PEACH 2

NECTARINE 2

LIME JUICE
1 TSP

SUGAR TO
TASTE

MINT 5G

Fruit Salad with Cucumber

GREEN
APPLE 2

WHITE
GRAPES 200G

ORANGE 2

LEMON 1/4

CUCUMBER 1

SUGAR 50G

VANILLA
POD 1/2

Fruit Salad with Grape Seed Oil

PERSIMMON 3

TANGERINE 3

GRAPEFRUIT 1/2

POMEGRANATE 1/2

GRAPE SEED OIL 1TBSP.

HONEY 2 TSP.

GROUND BLACK PEPPER TO TASTE

Fruit Salad with Watermelon & Plums

PLUM 6

HONEY TO TASTE

CINNAMON TO TASTE

WATERMELON 300G

Fruit Salad with Sweet Coconut Flakes

PINEAPPLE
400G

MANGO 300G

KIWI 3

RED
GRAPES 150G

CARAMBOLA
1

HONEY 3
TBSP.

SWEET
COCONUT
FLAKES 4
TBSP.

LIME JUICE
1TBSP.

21

Chickpea Sprouts Salad

WALNUT 50G

ONION 1

HONEY 1TSP.

SOY SAUCE 1TSP.

OLIVE OIL 2 TBSP.

MUSTARD 1TSP.

SALT TO TASTE

GREEN APPLE 1

GREEN SALAD 2 BUNCHES

CHICKPEA /SPROUT/50 G

Winter Fruit Salad

POMEGRANATE 1

PAPAYA 1

APPLE 2

BANANA 1

DATES 5

FIG 2

RED GRAPES 50G

PERSIMMON 1

MultiColored Fruit Salad with Prunes

ORANGE 3

BANANA 2

KIWI 1

PRUNES 5

WALNUT 50G

HONEY
3 TBSP.

LEMON
JUICE 1 TSP.

 ——————————

Fruit Salad with Red Cabbage

RED
CABBAGE 1/4

POMEGRANATE
1

APPLE 1

ORANGE 1

WALNUT 50G

HONEY
1 TBSP.

BALSAMIC
VINEGAR 1/2
TBSP.

LIVE OIL
2TBSP.

ROUND
BLACK
PEPPER TO
TASTE

SALT TO
TASTE

Fruit Salad with Melon & Pineapple

PINEAPPLE 350G

MELON 350G

STRAWBERRY 250G

MINT 15G

BASIL TO TASTE

SOUR CREAM 200G

Fruit Salad with Avocado & Pistachios

ORANGE 300G

CANTALOUPE 1

AVOCADO 1

MINT 10G

LIME JUICE 1/2 TBSP.

SOUR CREAM TO TASTE

GROUND PISTACHIOS TO TASTE

Fruit Salad "Fantasy"

PEAR 1

APPLE 1

ORANGE 1

BANANA 1

PEACH 1

KIWI 1

WALNUT 100G

WHIPPED CREAM TO TASTE

Fruit Salad with Pomegranate & Persimmon

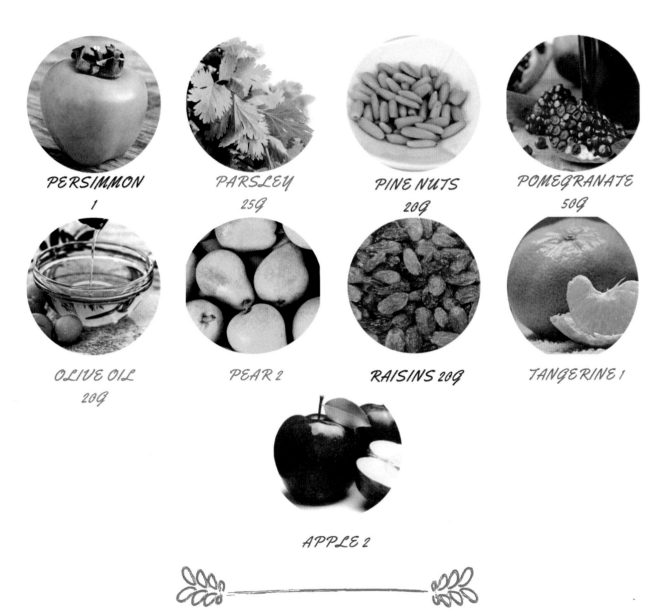

PERSIMMON
1

PARSLEY
25G

PINE NUTS
20G

POMEGRANATE
50G

OLIVE OIL
20G

PEAR 2

RAISINS 20G

TANGERINE 1

APPLE 2

Fruit Salad with Canned Pineapple

BANANA 2

APPLE 2

RED GRAPES 80G

WHITE GRAPES 80G

SUGAR 1TBSP

ORANGE JUICE 1TBSP

LEMON JUICE 1/2TBSP.

CANNED PINEAPPLE 200G

Fruit Salad with Walnuts & Honey

APPLE 3   ORANGE 3   WALNUT TO   HONEY TO
                                   TASTE   TASTE

Fruit Salad with Couscous

BLUEBERRY
100G

NECTARINE 2

COUSCOUS
300G

SALT TO
TASTE

OLIVE OIL
2TBSP.

ORANGE
JUICE
2TBSP.

GROUND
BLACK
PEPPER TO
TASTE

GROUND
ALMONDS
2TBSP

Fruit Salad with Orange & Passionfruit

ORANGE 2

PASSION FRUIT 2

SUGAR 1/2 TBSP.

GOOSEBERRY TO TASTE

Fruit Salad with Strawberries & Kiwi

STRAWBERRY
500G

KIWI 2

SOUR
CREAM 200G

SUGAR
2TBSP.

POWDERED
SUGAR
1TBSP.

Fruit salad "Wonderful"

PERSIMMON 2

PEAR 2

ORANGE 1

LEMON 1/2

BANANA 1

POMEGRANATE 1

HONEY 3TBSP.

KIWI 1

APPLE 1

Fruit Salad with Chia Seeds

APPLE 1

BANANA 3

KIWI 1

RAISINS 50G

DRIED
DATES 70G

CHIA SEEDS
2 TSP.

YOGURT 150G

LEMON
JUICE 1
TBSP.

COCONUT
FLAKES
2 TSP.

Fruit salad with Mango, Pineapple & Peach

CANNED
PINEAPPLE
100G

PEACH 2

HONEY 1TSP.

LEMON
JUICE
1TBSP.

MANGO 1

Fruit Salad with Strawberries & Orange

ORANGE 2

GRAPEFRUIT 1

BANANA 1

STRAWBERRY 250G

BLUEBERRY TO TASTE

ORANGE JUICE TO TASTE

38

Fruit Salad with Green Peppers & Hazelnuts

PEAR 2

GRAPEFRUIT 1

VEGETABLE OIL 2TBSP.

SALT TO TASTE

GREEN PEPPER 1

PARSLEY 50G

HAZELNUT 50G

GREEN SALAD TO TASTE

Fruit Salad with Quince

QUINCE 2

APPLE 2

PRUNES
100G

KIWI 1

POWDERED
SUGAR TO
TASTE

SOUR
CREAM TO
TASTE

PISTACHIOS
50G

Salad with Orange, Spinach & Avocado

SPINACH
180G

ORANGE 1

AVOCADO 1

GINGER
ROOT 10G

VEGETABLE
OIL 1 TBSP.

SALT TO
TASTE

GROUND
BLACK
PEPPER TO
TASTE

Spinach, Orange & Turnip Salad

SPINACH
180G

ORANGE 3

TURNIP 3

HONEY
2TBSP.

LIME 1TBSP.

OLIVE OIL
3TBSP.

AVOCADO 1

PARSLEY
50G

RED ONION
1/2

SALT TO
TASTE

Melon, Lime & Mint Salad

LIME 1

MELON 1KG

MINT 3 TBSP.

SUGAR
1 TSP.

GINGER
ROOT 1 TSP.

HONEY
1 TBSP.

Salad with Oranges, Tomatoes & Celery

TOMATO 500G

ORANGE 3

OLIVE OIL
50G

CELERY 100G

GARLIC
1TSP.

PARSLEY
20G

RED ONION 1

SALT TO
TASTE

Papaya with Lime Juice, Honey, Mint & Basil

PAPAYA 1

HONEY
2TBSP.

LIME 1/2

MINT 10G

BASIL 30G

Mango & Sea Bass Salad

MANGO 100G

SEA BASS
FILLET 60G

RUCOLA 20G

LEMON
JUICE 1TSP.

OLIVE OIL
1TBSP.

 ——————————

Celery Salad with Green Apple

CELERY
STALK 4

GREEN
APPLE 1

MAYONNAISE
2 TBSP.

SALT TO
TASTE

Strawberry & Cherry Salad

STRAWBERRY 200G

RUCOLA 50G

OLIVE OIL 2TBSP.

SALT TO TASTE

CHERRY TOMATOES 150G

MOZZARELLA 100G

BALSAMIC VINEGAR 1TSP.

Banana, Apple & Celery Salad

BANANA 2

APPLE 2

CELERY 200G

YOGURT 100G

MELISSA 30G

Salad with Cabbage, Carrots & Pineapple

CABBAGE 400G

CARROT 300G

CANNED PINEAPPLE 200G

MAYONNAISE 3 TBSP.

Celery & Apple Salad

CELERY
STALK 3

GREEN
APPLE 1

COTTAGE
CHEESE 200G

YOGURT 200G

Salad with Pear, Celery & Pecans

CELERY
STALK 4

APPLE
VINEGAR
2TBSP.

HONEY
2TBSP.

SALT TO
TASTE

PEAR 2

GROUND
PECANS
4TBSP

CHEDDAR
CHEESE 200G

LETTUCE
LEAVES 6

 ——————————

Pineapple Salad with Avocado & Red Onion

PINEAPPLE 1

AVOCADO 1

CILANTRO 20G

RED ONION 1

OLIVE OIL 2TBSP.

SALT TO TASTE

WHITE WINE VINEGAR 1TBSP.

GROUND BLACK PEPPER TO TASTE

Spinach Salad with Pear & Avocado

LIME JUICE
1TSP.

CILANTRO
1TSP.

GARLIC
1/4TSP.

SPINACH
170G

PEAR 1

AVOCADO 1

RED ONION
1/2

GORGONZOLA
CHEESE 50G

OLIVE OIL
2TBSP.

Fruit Breakfast with Nuts

BANANA 2

WALNUT
250G

APPLE 1

YOGURT 200G

HONEY
1TBSP.

Orange & Avocado Salad

ORANGE 1

AVOCADO 1

FENNEL 1/2

GREEN SALAD 100G

LEMON JUICE TO TASTE

SALT TO TASTE

GROUND BLACK PEPPER TO TASTE

PINE NUTS 50G

Broccoli & Apple Salad

BOILED
BROCCOLI
350G

RED APPLE
1

ALMOND 40G

HONEY 1TSP.

RED ONION
1/2

LEMON
JUICE
2TBSP.

OLIVE OIL
3TBSP.

SALT TO
TASTE

Summer Salad with Ham & Apples

CELERY 1

CUCUMBER 1

APPLE 1

HAM 150G

GREEN SALAD 100G

MAYONNAISE 50G

ORANGE JUICE 2TBSP.

SALT TO TASTE

Salad with Watermelon, Feta & Mint

WATERMELON
300G

CHEESE
FETA 400G

OLIVE OIL
3 TBSP.

SALT TA
TASTE

PINE NUTS
TO TASTE

MINT 20G

Chicken Salad with Fruits & Nuts

SALT TO TASTE

APPLE 1

GROUND WALNUT 40G

RAISINS 2TBSP.

RED GRAPES 150G

MAYONNAISE 2TBSP.

YOGURT 1TBSP.

LEMON JUICE 1TBSP.

FRIED CHICKEN BREAST FILLET 2

Shrimp & Tangerine Salad

TANGERINE 6

SHRIMP 150G

CELERY
STALK 100G

APPLE 1

MAYONNAISE
3 TBSP.

GREEN
SALAD TO
TASTE

SALT TO
TASTE

LEMON
JUICE
1 TBSP.

Strawberry, Peach & Melon Salad

PEACH 1

STRAWBERRY
150G

MELON 100G

RASPBERRY
50G

SUGAR 50G

LIME JUICE
2TBSP

BLACKBERRY
50G

MINT 15G

BLACK CURRANT
50G

Chicken Salad with Mango, Cucumber & Red Pepper

LEMON JUICE
2TBSP.

MAYONNAISE
1TBSP.

MUSTARD
2TSP.

MUSTARD...

SALT TO
TASTE

OLIVE OIL
2TBSP.

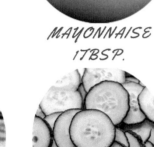
CUCUMBER 1

RED
PEPPER 1

MANGO 1

FRIED CHICKEN
BREAST FILLET 2

RED ONION 1

CHIVES
2TSP.

LETTUCE
250G

Melon Salad

CANTALOUPE
200G

PARMA HAM
100G

RUCOLA 100G

LEMON 1/2

OLIVE OIL
2TBSP.

SALT TO
TASTE

Pepper & Peach Salad

PEACH 3

RED
PEPPER 3

OLIVE OIL
2TBSP.

LEMON
JUICE
2TBSP.

SULGUNI
CHEESE 200G

PARSLEY
20G

DILL 20G

SALT TO
TASTE

Salad with Celery, Apples & Walnuts

CELERY
STALK 300G

APPLE 200G

WALNUT
130G

LEMON 1/4

MAYONNAISE
3 TBSP.

Pineapple Salad with Fresh Fruit Mix

PINEAPPLE 1

APPLE 2

GRAPES 200G

MANGO 1

ORANGE 2

KIWI 2

POMEGRANATE 1

OLIVE OIL 2TBSP.

HONEY 1TBSP.

Salad with Apricots & Cherry Tomatoes

CHERRY TOMATOES 100G

APRICOT 3

DRIED FIGS 3

WALNUT 50G

OLIVE OIL 1TBSP.

BALSAMIC VINEGAR 2TSP.

PARMESAN CHEESE 50G

LETTUCE 100G

Cucumber Salad with Fresh Herbs & Orange

ORANGE 2

CUCUMBER 5

OLIVE OIL
2 TBSP.

LEMON 1/2

ROSEMARY
1 TBS.

FRESH
OREGANO
LEAVES
1 TSP.

MINT 1 TBSP.

SALT TO
TASTE

Currant with Honey

BLACK
CURRANT
75G

RED
CURRANT
75G

WHITE
CURRENT
75G

HONEY
2TBSP

ORANGE 1

Apple & Pineapple Salad

APPLE 1

CANNED
PINEAPPLE
250G

CELERY
STALK 150G

WALNUT 50G

MAYONNAISE
1TBSP.

Mango & Pineapple Salad

MANGO 1

PINEAPPLE
200G

CHERRY
TOMATOES
150G

RED
PEPPER 1

SESAME
SEEDS 50G

OLIVE OIL
2TBSP.

CUCUMBER 1

Ham & Melon Salad

RUCOLA 100G

PARMA HAM 100G

MELON 200G

LEMON JUICE 1TBSP.

OLIVE OIL 3TBSP.

SALT TO TASTE

Watermelon & Radish Salad

WATERMELON
300G

LIME JUICE
1TSP.

OLIVE OIL
1TBSP.

MINT 20G

CILANTRO
1TBSP.

RUCOLA 30G

RADISH 2

CAPERS
1TBSP.

ROASTED
PEANUTS
2TBSP.

SALT TO
TASTE

Watermelon Salad with Feta Cheese

GREEN
SALAD 150G

WATERMELON
250G

FETA
CHEESE 100G

OLIVE OIL
2TBSP.

LEMON 1/2

PINE NUTS
50G

BASIL 50G

SALT TO
TASTE

Pear & Pancetta Salad

HONEY
1TBSP.

WHITE WINE
VINEGAR
1TBSP.

LEMON
JUICE 1TSP.

SALT TO
TASTE

OLIVE OIL
3TBSP.

PANCETTA
100G

PEAR 1

RUCOLA 150G

Cabbage Salad

CABBAGE
150G

WHITE
GRAPES 100G

HONEY
1TBSP.

ORANGE 2

LEMON
JUICE
1TBSP.

APPLE 1

SUNFLOWER
SEEDS
2TBSP.

77

Watermelon Salad with Rum & Mint

LIME JUICE
1 TBSP.

SUGAR 1 TBSP.

RUM 1 TBSP.

WATERMELON
1KG

MINT 2 TBSP.

Mango & Parma Ham Salad

CHERRY
TOMATOES 8

MOZZARELLA
150G

GREEN
SALAD 100G

RUCOLA 50G

PARMA HAM
75G

MANGO 1

PESTO 2 TSP.

OLIVE OIL
3 TBSP.

MUSTARD
1 TSP.

BALSAMIC
VINEGAR 2 TBSP.

SALT TO
TASTE

Olives & Orange Salad

ORANGE 1

CHERRY
TOMATOES 4

OLIVE OIL
1TBSP.

SALT TO
TASTE

GREEN
SALAD 100G

OLIVES 50G

Mushroom, Apple & Orange Salad

FRESH
CHAMPIGNON
MUSHROOMS
10

ORANGE 1

APPLE 2

OLIVE OIL
50ML

CHEDDAR
CHEESE
200G

SALT TO
TASTE

LEMON
JUICE
1TBSP

Chicken Salad with Oranges & Pomegranate

ORANGE 1

POMEGRANATE 1/2

CHEESE TO TASTE 100G

APPLE 2

SOUR CREAM 100G

SALT TO TASTE

GREEN SALAD 50G

BOILED CHICKEN BREAST FILLET 400G

Salad with Orange & Mint

GREEN
SALAD 100G

ORANGE 2

ORANGE
JUICE 2 TBSP.

LEMON JUICE
1 TBSP.

SALT TO
TASTE

VEGETABLE
OIL 1 TBSP.

GROUND BLACK
PEPPER TO
TASTE

MINT 10 G

Green Salad

GREEN
SALAD 100G

STRAWBERRY
150G

PHYSALIS
150G

ORANGE 1

APPLE 1

MINT 50G

Green Salad with Orange & Avocado

GREEN
SALAD 500G

ORANGE 3

AVOCADO 1

RED ONION
50G

OLIVE OIL
3TBSP

Celery & Fruit Salad

GREEN
SALAD 100G

KIWI 1

APPLE 1

CHINESE
CABBAGE
100G

CELERY
STALK 3

SALT TO
TASTE

OLIVE OIL
2TBSP.

Salad with Pear & Cashews

PEAR 1

WATERCRESS
150G.

RUCOLA 100G

GREEN
SALAD 200G

CASHEW
NUTS 4 TBSP.

VEGETABLE
OIL 1 TBSP.

SOY SAUCE
1 TBSP.

LIME JUICE
1 TBSP.

Rucola & Avocado Salad

RUCOLA 200G

AVOCADO 1

CHERRY
TOMATOES
100G

OLIVE OIL
2TBSP.

BALSAMIC
VINEGAR 1TSP.

SALT TO
TASTE

Artichoke & Orange Salad

ARTICHOKE 1

RUCOLA 50G

ORANGE 1

RED ONION 1

LEMON JUICE
2 TBSP.

OLIVE OIL
2 TBSP.

SALT TO
TASTE

GROUND BLACK
PEPPER TO
TASTE

Salad with Spinach, Pear & Nuts

SPINACH 100G

GREEN SALAD 100G

PINE NUTS 20G

CASHEW NUTS 20G

ALMOND 20G

HAZELNUT 20G

WALNUT 20G

SOY SAUCE 1TBSP.

HONEY 3TBSP.

DORBLU CHEESE 100G

MUSTARD 1TBSP.

PEAR 2

Pumpkin & Apple Salad

PUMPKIN 500

LEMON 1

APPLE 3

HONEY
3 TBSP.

NUTS TO
TASTE 3 TBSP.

Artichoke & Pear Salad

SHRIMP 150G

SALT TO TASTE

PEAR 60G

CHERRY TOMATOES 50G

GREEN SALAD 50G

CANNED ARTICHOKES 50G

OLIVE OIL 1TBSP.

ORANGE JUICE 1TBSP.

Avocado Salad with Sunflower Seeds

TOMATO 2

CUCUMBER 2

AVOCADO 1

RED ONION 1/2

GREEN SALAD 100G

OLIVE OIL 2TBSP.

MUSTARD 1/2TSP.

BALSAMIC VINEGAR 1TBSP.

SUNFLOWER SEEDS 4TBSP.,

SALT TO TASTE

Lettuce, Radish & Pine Nuts Salad

RADISH 6

PINE NUTS
30G

LETTUCE
450G

OLIVE OIL
2TBSP.

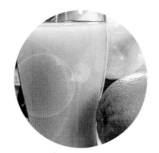

ORANGE
JUICE 1TBSP.

LEMON
JUICE 1TBSP.

94

Carrot, Orange & Cinnamon Salad

CARROT 3

ORANGE 2

SALT TO TASTE

CINNAMON TO TASTE

NUTMEG TO TASTE

POWDERED SUGAR 2TBSP.

OLIVE OIL 3TBSP.

Salad with Cucumber, Pineapple & Peanuts

PINEAPPLE
1/2

SCALLION
50G

CUCUMBER 1

MINT 1TBSP.

GREEN
PEPPER 1

LIME JUICE
1TBSP.

SUGAR
1TSP.

ROASTED
PEANUTS 120G

OLIVE OIL
1TBSP.

Cabbage Salad with Oranges & Herbs

BASIL 50G

ORANGE 2

PARSLEY 50G

SCALLION 50G

OLIVE OIL 2 TBSP.

SALT TO TASTE

WHITE CABBAGE 300G

Citrus Salad with Cardamom

GRAPEFRUIT
1

ORANGE 3

HONEY
2TBSP.

LIME JUICE
2TBSP.

GROUND
CARDAMOM
1/4TSP.

Made in the USA
Las Vegas, NV
15 October 2023

79167917R00062